'A fascinating account of the achievements of John White, the Dorchester Rector who played a vital role in helping the persecuted escape from King Charles's England to the New World. He is one of the true founding fathers of America and his story deserves to be commemorated on both sides of the Atlantic.'

Julian Fellowes

DORCHESTER'S NEW WORLD

DORCHESTER'S NEW WORLD

THE VISION OF JOHN WHITE,
'FOUNDER OF MASSACHUSETTS'

DAVID CUCKSON

YOUCAXTON PUBLICATIONS
OXFORD & SHREWSBURY

David Cuckson studied law and theology at the University of Cambridge. He has worked as a Congregational/ United Reformed Church minister and as a solicitor in local government and in private practice. He is now retired and lives in Dorchester.

ISBN 978-1-911175-64-3
Printed and bound in Great Britain.
Published by YouCaxton Publications 2017

YouCaxton Publications
enquiries@youcaxton.co.uk

Foreword

John White was rector of Dorchester from 1605 until his death in 1648. A devout Anglican and scholar, he lived through turbulent times and his sympathies espoused Puritan ideals. Initially his ideas for reform were unpopular but after the great fire of 1613, his compassion and wise ministry won the respect of the townsfolk and he led them to reform the whole social structure and government of the town.

The increasing persecution of Puritans in England inspired his vision to found a colony in New England where people would be free to practise their beliefs as they could not in Dorchester. Although White himself never visited America he helped found the Dorchester Company and later the Massachusetts Bay Company that were instrumental in supporting the first emigrants from Dorset, Somerset and Devon in the 1630s. Had it not been for his determination and influence the settlements would probably have failed from starvation, disease and cold. Here we can read of the courage and privations of these first settlers in fascinating detail. Not for nothing was he known as the Father of Massachusetts.

Today John White is largely forgotten, so I welcome this little book which reminds us of this remarkable character and of life in Dorchester during the early 17th century including the Civil War. The medieval rectory where John White lived with his wife and four children still stands and is now owned by Dorset County Museum. This is about to be restored and converted into a new learning centre as part of a multimillion pound development of the museum.

Dr Peter Down, Chairman of the Board of Trustees of the Dorset Natural History and Archaeological Society

Acknowledgements

This book owes its origins to a live trans-Atlantic link-up between Dorchester, Dorset and Dorchester, Massachusetts, arranged by the Dorset County Museum, for which I helped prepare some display panels about John White and his contribution to both communities. Since then I have appreciated the encouragement and support from a number of people, both staff and volunteers, at the Museum. This includes the right to use images from the Museum's resources. I hope that it will not be too long before readers of this book will be able to go inside a revamped interior of the building in which John White lived with his family, as it is incorporated in the current redevelopment and extension of the Museum's premises.

The only contemporary image thought probably to be of John White is both dark and unclear, and I am very grateful to Jo Duncan for bringing him to life in her drawing and for allowing me to reproduce this here.

Contents

Contents

Part 1

A New World at Home

1

John White, Puritan Preacher

In November 1605 Dorchester welcomed a new Rector to the town. The Reverend John White came with first-rate academic qualifications, having spent the previous five years as a fellow of New College, Oxford. So, he was first and foremost a scholar, a student of theology, but his understanding of the Christian faith meant that he was very concerned as to how this faith was expressed in everyday living. He would have been categorised as one of those church people known as 'Puritans'.

This was the time of King James I, a period that saw the publication of the Authorised Version of the Bible, a new official translation of the whole of the Bible into English, based on the best scholarship of the time. James had been brought up in Scotland as a Protestant, a follower of the Reformation led by such people as Martin Luther, who protested about the state of the Church of his day, and John Calvin, who introduced new forms of church government and worship in the city of Geneva. It looked as though England might become a strongly Protestant country, as Scotland had already done. Henry VIII's break with the Roman Catholic Church had been more to do with escaping foreign control (especially control by the Pope) over church affairs in England, and it was only when his son succeeded him as Edward VI that there was a determined effort to introduce the Reformers' ideas into the Church of England. Queen Mary, of course, tried to reverse this trend, and it was left to Queen Elizabeth to try to steer a middle course in order to hold the nation together. This did mean, however, that some leading Roman Catholics were imprisoned and even executed as a threat to the state (as commemorated by the Dorset Martyrs Memorial on Gallows Hill in Dorchester). Action was also taken against some of the more radical Protestants, and this lead some to leave the country, perhaps initially to the Netherlands where they found greater freedom, and then, as Pilgrim Fathers on *the Mayflower*, to emigrate to the New World of America.

John White was comfortable with how the Church of England was at the time of his arrival in Dorchester. Some of the reforms introduced here, such as moving the altar from its position at the east end of the church to become a communion table closer to the congregation, and a simpler style of worship, reflected his own preferences, and appear to have been readily accepted by the leading members of the congregations, who, after all, will have had some say in his selection as the new minister for the town. He was noted for his preaching, often at length, always based on Bible passages and echoing some of the ideas of John Calvin as to how the Bible should be interpreted. It was only after Charles I ascended the throne in 1625, and especially when Archbishop Laud tried to undo some of these 'puritan' reforms, insisting that all churches conform to a single pattern of worship, including the re-introduction of more ceremony, that John White found himself in difficulties. Some clergymen soon came into immediate conflict with the church authorities, but John White tried not to stir up trouble for the sake of it, and generally he did not challenge the way the Church of England was ordered, with its bishops and so on, as some Puritans did. However, when in 1633 Charles I issued a declaration, known as the 'Book of Sports', which encouraged people to engage in recreation, such as dancing and archery, on Sundays rather than just during the week, John White defied an order of the archbishop to read the declaration in church. The Puritans were against what they regarded as frivolous recreation being organised on Sundays. He was also reported for an outspoken sermon, which caused him to be investigated as a possible non-conformist. A search was made of his study at home for evidence against him, but, unlike a number of other ministers, he seems to have escaped punishment. Throughout this time he maintained his emphasis on studying the Bible and he encouraged his parishioners to do the same and to think about the implications of what they read for the daily life and the life of their town.

Dorchester had three churches at this time, all on the High Street. Holy Trinity, now a Roman Catholic Church, was linked with St Peter's, and John White was responsible for both. They acted as the parish churches for the upper part of the town, which is where the better-off people lived. Each church had a congregation of about 1,000 people. All Saints, now disused as a church and leased by the Dorset County Museum, served the poorer, lower part of the town (Fordington was then a separate village). John White later encouraged William Benn to come to Dorchester to work with him in ministering to the whole town and, after a short time, to take particular responsibility for All Saints. Benn was also a Puritan, in fact more radical than John White, and in the end he left the Church of England altogether, establishing what was to become the Congregational Church in Dorchester (now part of the United Church in South Street).

John White was part of the emerging middle class. His father leased the manor of Stanton St John from New College, Oxford, through the favour of a relation, Dr Thomas White, who was for a time Warden of New College. John was born in 1575. He was educated at Winchester College, before going on to New College himself. In 1606, shortly after his arrival in Dorchester, John married Anne Burges, the sister of a close friend of John's and fellow Puritan minister. They had four children, John, Samuel, Josiah and Nathaniel. We do not have any record of when Anne died, and it seems most likely that she died in London when they were living there at the time of the Civil War. The family lived in the Rectory in Colliton Street, a building that still survives, now incorporated into the premises of the Museum.

John White may well have hoped to live out his days ministering in his beloved Dorchester. But national events decreed otherwise. A festering dispute between Parliament and King Charles worsened to the point where, in 1642, the King decided to try to impose his will by force and raised his standard at Nottingham, an act which formally began the Civil War. People up and down the country found that they had to choose sides, and John White, together with most of the folk in Dorchester, opted to side with Parliament. The king ruled, they maintained, by the will of the common people, which for most practical purposes was represented by Parliament. Where the king sought, for example, to tax the people without seeking the ratification of Parliament, he should be brought back into line. So when the king raised an army, Parliament decided to resist and ensured that it had forces under its control.

Dorchester became the headquarters for the Parliamentary forces in Dorset. Some efforts were made to defend the town, but in June 1643 there was general panic when news came that a strong Royalist force was only 12 miles away, at Blandford, whereas the back-up Parliamentary army was engaged elsewhere. Dorchester was left to its own devices and the local leaders decided to seek the best terms they could for the surrender of the town. The usual assurances were given as to the safety of people and property, and, as usual too, ignored by some. John White had already left the town, but his library of books, which must have meant so much to a scholar like himself, was plundered by the Royalist cavalry.

The reason why John White was away was that he had been called by Parliament to join what became known as the 'Westminster Assembly of Divines'. This body, which included leading Puritans within the Church, both clergymen and lay people, was designed to be consulted in relation to, and to make recommendations on, the future government of the Church. He was described by a contemporary as 'one of the wisest and most learned' among the members of the Assembly, and he was asked to chair one of the committees. This concerned itself with a review of the ministers in the London and Hertfordshire area, to identify those associated with the High Church party which followed Archbishop Laud – these ministers were ejected from their livings and replaced with ministers more in tune with the Puritan sympathies of the Parliamentarians. In the light of the situation in Dorchester John White was reluctant to return there yet, and he accepted an appointment to the parish of Savoy in Lambeth, which carried with it the use of the ejected minister's library 'until his own should be returned'.

John White was now over 70 years old, and he was finding full-time ministry an increasing strain. He spoke once of being 'distracted ... by pain and grief' (perhaps, in part, the death of his wife). By November 1646 he decided that it would be best for him to return to Dorchester, to live out his last days. The First Civil War was over and the Parliamentarians were mostly in control of the country, although a couple of years later the King would make another bid to recover power, an exercise that was to end with his trial and execution. Dorchester, however, was not the place it was. The parishes had been impoverished by the war and, although the Corporation helped out to a limited extent, John White was beset with financial difficulties. More seriously, the people were no longer united behind their minister. In addition to a significant minority of Royalist sympathisers, an increasing number of people were being attracted by some of the radical sects that had proliferated during the chaos of civil war, including one that claimed that there was no sin and that to the godly all things were pure, even drunkenness, blasphemy and fornication; John White tried to counter these 'heresies' and in March 1647 he held a special Fast at St Peter's. Efforts were made to find an assistant for the elderly minister, but before one could be found he died, on 21 July 1648. He was buried in the church porch of St Peter's, where a plaque has been put up in his memory. For the funeral and for a month afterwards the porch was draped in black as a sign of mourning.

2

'Fire from Heaven'

At the beginning of the seventeenth century Dorchester was a town of about 2,000 people. It was still confined by the line of the old Roman walls, today marked out by West Walks, South Walks and Icen Way. It had status as the county and assize town, and was also a parliamentary borough. People came from miles around to its markets, to buy goods from its butchers, bakers, chandlers, shoemakers and tradesmen of every kind. There was a Free School in South Street, offering a good education to its students, and grateful to Thomas Hardye for his financial endowment (now commemorated in the school's name). There was also a thriving cloth industry, not just weavers but also master clothiers. It benefited from its proximity to the port of Weymouth to enjoy trade with France and the wider continent. A couple of merchant families had done so well in the sixteenth century that they had moved up into the ranks of the gentry. These were the Williamses and the Churchills, who still retained an interest in property in the town during our period. Just outside the town, at Wolfeton House, lived the Trenchards, a notable Protestant family, with the Russells, raised up to be Earls of Bedford, exercising general patronage, in particular over the selection of Members of Parliament.

A lot of the people in the town, however, were very poor, and the extent of the poverty led to a constant threat of disorder. The population had grown rapidly as people moved in from the countryside around, looking for work, and there was also a growth in the birth rate. There was not enough work for everyone, and the number of unemployed and disaffected youths created particular problems in the streets. Some of this might have been put down to high spirits, but idleness coupled with poverty led to petty theft within the town and also the stealing of food from the surrounding fields. With little else to look forward to, many turned to drink, and drunkenness became the greatest threat to good order. Fighting would break out in the streets, and there was a general loosening of morals. Adultery became more common, and there were also cases of rape. The institution of the family, which had been the mainstay of social life, was being challenged, with neglected children and battered wives. The 'deserving poor' were helped from the parish rates, but this assistance was haphazard in its application. The Corporation was ruled by burgesses who had little interest in improving the lot of the poor, or even in encouraging mutual help and charity on any systematic basis.

The kinds of recreation indulged in by the poor were seen by the Puritans as making matters worse. Bear-baiting and bull-baiting brought men together in a competitive environment, and even the Fairs and the Maypole dance were treated as excuses for much drinking. These activities were tolerated and even encouraged by many of the leading citizens as an easy way of appeasing those who were otherwise being oppressed and exploited. And if this kind of recreation took place on a Sunday, then that freed up time in the rest of the week for work, although there was a potential clash with the laws that made attendance at worship in the Church of England compulsory. These laws were primarily directed against Roman Catholics and members of extreme Protestant sects who objected to Church of England worship, but they also caught those who missed the services because of participation in sports or, equally, because of hangovers from the day before. It was the difficulty of separating the festive events from the associated drunkenness that led the Puritans to try to ban the events altogether. This extended even to the celebration of Christmas, where some treated the Twelve Days of Christmas as an excuse for continuous raucous partying.

The Puritans in general, and John White in particular when he began his ministry in the town, tended to focus first on the symptoms before turning to deal with the underlying causes, highlighting the 'sins' and calling on the people to repent and reform their ways. This tended to make them unpopular, not just with the poor, but also with some of the better-off citizens, who had done well out of society as it was, often by exploiting those less fortunate than themselves. A typical attack was one of hypocrisy, and several of these were contained in anonymous 'libels', scurrilous verses dropped in the street or shop doorways mocking the Puritans. One such included the lines:-

> *You carry your bible God's word to expound*
> *And yet in all knavery you daily abound . . .*
> *Yea, covetousness, lechery and lying for gain*
> *Amongst you Puritans is not counted vain.*

They also mocked the Puritans, including John White by name, for their belief, following the teaching of John Calvin, that some Christians are 'the elect', chosen by God to be saved out of the population at large. A distorted view of this belief is expressed by the libeller in the following lines:-

> *Having myself heard a sermon now of late*
> *preached in the church by a puritan prelate . . .*
> *The Saviour of the world, Christ Jesus in person*
> *of his famed death was brought in question*
> *How that he was not the saviour of us all,*
> *but of the elected which can never fall.*

There was a strong suspicion, though never proved, that the person behind these libels was Matthew Chubb. He was the leading citizen in the town, as well as being the wealthiest. Over time he held all the important civic offices and he was also Member of Parliament for a period. He had various business concerns including, it was alleged, money-lending at usurious rates of interest. His acts of generosity tended to be limited to his family and his close friends and associates, people who would serve his interests, or where a gift would enhance his standing in the town. Later, after the fire, he made play of a gift of £500 to help rebuild the town, but this was done against an understanding that he would be given the sum of £1,000 for the purpose by the King (though it must be said that there was a high risk that he would never actually receive this). Later on still, his widow would leave money to help endow Chubb's almshouse for women.

Matthew Chubb hated John White and all that he stood for in terms of churchmanship, even to the point that on a Sunday morning he would walk across the fields to the service at the church in Fordington rather than attend his parish church in Dorchester. He was also said to have offered £100 if someone could get White to leave the town. On the other hand he seems to have provided a degree of protection, and sometimes shelter in his house, for a local Roman Catholic, Robert Adyn, who was constantly stirring up trouble and who was strongly suspected as being the actual author of the libels directed against John White. Chubb and White would never have seen eye to eye, and it was only the intervention of third parties that led to a formal reconciliation. It is a sign as to how far the relationship between the Rector and the leading burgess of the town had broken down that it took a written document, sealed in the presence of witnesses, to reduce the tensions to a tolerable level.

Such was the town in August 1613, and life might have continued much the same. But on 6 August, soon after two o'clock, a building caught fire. The fire seems to have been caused when a chandler named Baker, in his shop close to St Peter's church, was melting tallow. The fire under the kettle was too hot and the tallow blazed up, and then the whole house went up in flames. The weather had been hot and dry, and there was a strong breeze blowing that day. As in the Great Fire of London some fifty years later the fire spread quickly to adjoining buildings, most of which were constructed out of timber and thatch. Even then disaster might have been averted if there had been people about to fight the fire, but nearly everyone was out in the fields surrounding the town helping with the harvest. This was the busiest time of the year, with those that could getting paid work, and the rest out gleaning, following on and picking up what left-overs they could find lying on the ground.

As soon as the smoke and flames became visible to those outside in the fields everyone hurried back as quickly as they could. People were rushing about calling for water. The first priority was to go to the Shire Hall, just up the High Street from where the fire started. Under the Shire Hall lay the powder magazine, where forty barrels of gunpowder were stored, and these had to be got out to safety, to avoid an enormous explosion. So all efforts were directed to wrapping the barrels in wet sheets and rolling them upwind, out of the town and into the fields.

Only then did folk concentrate on the burning buildings. Even then, many of the owners thought only of taking out as many of their possessions as they could, leaving their homes behind them to burn. And so the fire spread. The wind seems to have been blowing from the west, because the worst of the devastation was suffered down into the High East Street area, around All Saints church. The County Gaol was down there, and the prisoners were released on the understanding that they would help fight the fires. It says something for their efforts that the gaol was saved and several prisoners, both men and women, later received royal pardons both for what they had done and for what they did not do, namely try to escape.

Help also came from villagers living outside the town and eventually the fires were brought under control and died down. 170 houses were lost, about half the number in the town. Of the churches, St Peter's and All Saints suffered damage but were soon repaired, while Holy Trinity seems to have escaped almost unscathed. This was remarkable, since the George Inn, which stood between Holy Trinity and St Peter's was completely gutted. Just one person, Cicely Bingham, an old woman, died in the fire.

Someone in the following autumn and winter wrote sadly that 'Dorchester was a famous town, now a heap of ashes for travellers to sigh at'. Most of the buildings were rebuilt or repaired fairly quickly, although even in 1621 there was a reference in a will to a vacant plot of land 'on which there was a house burnt down by the late fire'. John White's Rectory seems to have been damaged, because someone in the town gave him two pounds 'towards the edifying of his house'. The cost of all this, including the loss of possessions, was considerable. One estimate put the cost at £200,000, though the real figure is probably less than half this, but still a heavy burden in the days when there was no insurance. To pay out £350 or £400 on rebuilding a property was a big hit even for reasonably wealthy citizens, especially when they had also lost valuable stock and furnishings. At least one merchant, John Watts, a member of the Corporation and presumably a man of some substance, was 'much impoverished' by the destruction of his premises adjoining the Antelope yard and, after finding himself still unable to fund rebuilding two years later, sold the property to a local lawyer, Humphrey Joliffe.

Even when the houses had been rebuilt, the fire left its mark on those who had lived through it. More than sixty years later James Gould specifically mentioned in his will the two gold pieces that he had rescued from the ashes, and which he passed on to his son. The local diarist, William Whiteway, who was only fourteen in 1613, wrote of his recollection of 'great buildings turned into heaps of stones, into dust and ashes' and of 'the great miseries of many families that were in an instant harbourless'.

John White, as the leading minister of the town, sought to comfort his people but also to challenge them. Following the various biblical references to 'fire from heaven', he saw the destruction of so much of the town as a kind of wake-up call to the town. The immediate need was for people to help one another, both practically and financially, to rebuild their lives. More than that, however, they should change their priorities for all time. They should no longer rely on 'the fading quality of all these earthly things' but should set their hearts on 'the true treasure that shall not perish'. This was God's opportunity for a total reformation of the town, the creation of a godly community following the example of Calvin's Geneva. John White was an inspiring preacher and the majority of his congregations were in a mood to be inspired. He was giving them a lead, and an ideal to aim for, and they were ready to follow and to seek to make the ideal a reality.

3

A Reformed Town

Now, after the fire, John White had a much more receptive audience for his ideas as to how the lives of the people who made up his congregations and the life of the town itself could be transformed into a Christian commonwealth. 'Commonwealth' would later become the watchword for the new form of government for the whole nation, when King Charles was executed for his betrayal of his people and for a time there was no single person left to rule the people (until Oliver Cromwell seized control as Lord Protector). Dorchester was now to be a microcosm of what would later be the pattern sought by the Parliamentarians at Westminster. John White's vision was undoubtedly inspired by what he knew of John Calvin's reforms in Geneva, but building on the institutions that were already familiar to the folk in Dorchester. Not every idea was new and examples can be found elsewhere in England of particular aspects of the changes now being introduced. The end result, however, seen as a whole, was exceptional and marked Dorchester out as something very special.

In addition to the Sunday services John White worked hard to teach and care for the people in his town. There were services on other days in the week, he lectured three times a week, and on Friday mornings he progressively went through the Bible from beginning to end, interpreting the different passages and explaining their significance for his audience. This last programme took about six years to complete, after which he started again from the beginning.

Outside the immediate church environment he was often called on to mediate in disputes, both public and private. As part of his regular ministry he visited his parishioners in their homes, especially when any were sick or other need, to pray with them and to help them to a greater understanding of their faith.

Some time later he drew up a covenant, known as the 'Ten Vows', which can be seen as a formal expression of the vision that motivated him. He read the document out in a Saturday evening service before the monthly communion was held the next day, and the people were called on to assent to all the obligations with a great 'Amen' in unison. The first vow was to keep to the pure worship of God, without innovation or corruption; it is not expressly stated but presumably he means here worship free from both High Church or Roman Catholic elements and the wilder excesses of the radical protestant sects. Then there is the reading and meditating on the Scriptures, the instruction of children and families in the fear of the Lord, penitence for failings, both receiving and giving 'brotherly admonition' (the latter to be carried out sensitively), sorting out any differences with other people speedily, avoiding 'ways of gain adjudged scandalous by the godly-wise', looking for opportunities to spread the Gospel message both at home and abroad, caring for the afflicted by prayer and generous gifts (for example, food, clothing and practical help), and, finally, reviewing with one another how these vows are being fulfilled. Covenants of this kind became common in this period, and John White went on to encourage their use in the new settlements in America. They became in some places tests for continued participation in church, and even community, life, but John White preferred not to exclude those who would not give their assent to the Ten Vows, in the hope that they would come round in time to such a commitment.

John White needed the support of other ministers and assistants to help fulfil his ambitions for the town. However, money to pay for this was a problem. To date, the churches had relied heavily on endowments to pay their ministers. Holy Trinity was reasonably well off in this respect, with investments that produced about £60 a year, but St Peter's and All Saints each only had a fraction of that. There was a national body, called the Feoffees for Impropriations, that helped redistribute church income in favour of under-endowed parishes, and some of this money came to Dorchester. John White also persuaded his congregations to give 'very liberally', compared with how they had done earlier, and he also persuaded wealthy individuals, both locally and through his contacts in London, to give generously or to leave significant bequests in their wills. So, over the years, stipends for ministers were increased, which encouraged them to stay longer in the town.

The churches were now thriving in a way that they had not before. The shilling fine for non-attendance at Sunday worship, imposed by law in the time of Queen Elizabeth, was not always effective in getting everyone in church, but such evidence as there is suggests that Dorchester under John White's leadership saw virtually one hundred per cent attendance at communion by the adult population. There also seems to have been an improvement in the people's morality, to a degree which can only reflect the influence of the Church. The records of Holy Trinity parish show a sharp decline in the frequency of illegitimate births in the first half of the seventeenth century, and also a striking decline in the number of brides who were pregnant before they got married. There was a general improvement in the country at large, but the change in Dorchester was especially striking. Before 1611 in the Holy Trinity parish the illegitimacy rate was higher than the national average, whereas in the next decade it was less than half of that average, and in the early 1630s less than a quarter.

There was also a change in the government of the town. Implementation of law and order became more effective. The local law officers usually served for a year at a time. The most important of the lay officials were the constables, two of them up until 1619 and three thereafter. In earlier days these were often Members of the Corporation, but later tended to be younger, up-and-coming, men. They patrolled the town with the staffs of office, and were assisted by the watchmen. All male citizens were supposed to take their turn as watchmen, but the more wealthy often paid for substitutes. They walked round the town in pairs and were the first line of defence against violence and disorder, calling on the constables, with their stronger enforcement powers, as necessary. Their main targets were drunks, 'night walkers' (people out suspiciously late at night) and swearers. There is a story of watchmen one night hearing a violent domestic row going on in the home of Gabriel Butler, the barber-surgeon, in the course of which they heard him threaten to 'slit her nose or cut her throat'; the watchmen diligently continued to listen until they had counted thirty oaths before they intervened. The constables and watchmen were unpaid. They were assisted by the beadles and serjeants at mace, who were given modest payment, one or two pounds a year. The beadles were on duty during daylight hours, the watchmen covering the nights. The serjeants served warrants, collected fines, issued proclamations, and enforced market regulations, including checking that traders were not giving short weight.

Some offenders ended up in the County Gaol. These were primarily debtors and those awaiting trial at the county Sessions or the Assizes. Most of the prisoners were only locked up in cells at night and were otherwise able to walk relatively freely about the prison, even entertaining wives and other visitors. However, there were punishments for some, including 'hand-bolts' and other kinds of fetters, and carved above the gateway was an inscription warning those being taken inside of the ultimate sanction:-

Look in yourselves, this is the scope:
Sin brings prison, prison the rope.

Execution by hanging was carried out in public, and usually attracted a goodly crowd to gawp and jeer.

There was also the Blindhouse, next to St Peter's churchyard, which was the town lock-up, where drunks were put to sober up, and the House of Correction, or Bridewell, which was a cross between a workhouse and a prison. Bridewell was the destination for vagrants, runaway apprentices and the like, as well as sexual offenders. So a couple who arrived in the town from Somerset and falsely claimed to be married were committed there 'to be employed in labour and virtue'. Offenders might be made to beat hemp or make sack-cloth, and may also have been given a whipping.

Lesser punishments included the pillory, the stocks and the cucking-stool. The pillory held the offender standing up with his head and hands secured in the frame. The stocks, where the offender was seated and secured by the legs, were more generally used, sometimes where the offender was unable to pay a fine and most commonly for drunks (although the authorities tended to wait until the offender had sobered up before he was put in the stocks, so that he was fully aware of his shame, as well as for hygienic reasons). The cucking-stool was the traditional punishment for women convicted of scolding (which might be either verbal abuse or physical brawling between women). They were presumably 'plounced', the local term for a ducking, in the waters of the river Frome; there is a reference to one, presumably less serious, offence where the punishment was ordered to be deferred until 'the weather is warmer'.

The magistrates also acted from time to time as mediators, with regard to family breakdowns and disputes between servants and their masters. Those falling down on their family obligations might be let off with a warning, and ordered to mend their ways; one man, for example was ordered to pay a shilling a week to his aged father. A servant might be released from his or her contract of service if they were misused in some way.

Finally, the sidesmen and church-wardens were able to prosecute absentees, people who misbehaved in church or committed other offences under the Sunday observance laws. Offenders could be referred to the Archdeacon's Court at Blandford, but were more often dealt with locally.

Attempts to tackle the causes of drunkenness and disorder met with mixed results. Action was taken to close down unlicensed alehouses, with those running them being fined and given warnings of further action, but as one closed another seemed to open. There was more success in stopping theatrical productions, and travelling companies were banned from performing and told to leave the town. This was done even when their leader was able to produce a patent from the Master of the Revels, which allowed them to perform anywhere in the country. The local authorities risked incurring government intervention, but no-one in the town seems to have tried to stir things up against such bans. The only performances to be permitted were those staged by local scholars, which were usually edifying Latin comedies put on to impress the Bishop. 'Unlawful' games seems to have stopped altogether. Bowling ceased to take place on Bowling Alley Walk, though one person was prosecuted, albeit let off with a warning, for playing 'quoits on Whitsun Monday'.

John White understood the importance of 'training up the youth in time' in countering irresponsible behaviour. A positive reform to achieve this was the foundation of the Hospital. The founding deed noted that Dorchester contained 'great numbers of poor and needy people who lived by begging and dishonest courses'. The aim of the new institution was to provide for 'the training up and instructing the children of the poor in honest labour'. The Hospital could take fifty children at a time, who would be taught 'some lawful trade, mystery, or manual occupation'. They were also taught good conduct and morality. The local folk gave generously to its establishment and endowment; Margaret Chubb, Matthew's widow, gave £200. A building was acquired in South Street and a governor was appointed, a fustian weaver named John Coke. He was authorised to discipline the boys, but was not allowed to flog the girls, for whom a 'sober woman' was given the task of supervising (which included flogging at the whipping post when this was deemed necessary). The children were taught various crafts, including spinning and even bonelace-making (handmade lace made using bone bobbins), but this latter activity was stopped at the request of the local clothiers as being unfair competition. Adolescents up to the age of twenty-one were admitted, and parents sometimes petitioned for their children to be admitted, in the hope that this would give them a better start in life than if they had remained at home. Some of them went on to be apprentices. The moral and religious education was commonly done by 'catechising'; two or three times a week the children had to learn the questions and answers set out in a printed Catechism, which summarised the puritan approach to matters of faith, including the overriding importance of studying the Bible, Sunday observance, and obeying 'all superiors'.

In 1623 the general educational provision was enhanced by the establishment of an 'under school' for boys preparatory to their progressing to the Free School. There was no such place for girls, but boys from poor families had an opportunity to receive schooling of a reasonable standard. Apart from this there was no doubt some informal teaching going on, but at least here there was some elementary education in reading, as well as religion and discipline.

Money was coming in from various sources for different projects and charitable purposes and the question arose as to how it could be best invested. The old way had been to lend any surplus money to wealthy townsmen, at reasonable rates of interest admittedly, but still often giving the use of the money back to the original donors. By 1622 people were coming to the conclusion that there must be a better way of investing charitable funds, and the inspired solution was to build a municipal brewery. This had the double advantage of promising a reasonable profit and also of exercising a degree of control over the drink trade in the town, thus countering problems of drunkenness. The Brewhouse was built in the Hospital grounds and opened for business early in 1623. The enterprise thrived and soon became the biggest industrial operation in the town. Any surplus charitable funds were invested in the business, and it was even used as a kind of bank, there being records of money being deposited on the basis of being recoverable at a month's notice and of interest being paid on deposits.

The first call on the profits from the Brewhouse was the maintenance of the Hospital, both the keeping up of the buildings and the ongoing payment of wages and the costs of keeping the children. Other public expenditure, including the school and even some street repairs, was also assisted. Some gifts were made to the poor at Christmas and, for a time, it paid supplements for the ministers' stipends. All in all, it was a most successful operation.

Even the Brewhouse could not meet all the charitable needs of the town. The established system of poor relief also needed updating and strengthening. One of the problems in Dorchester was that All Saints parish contained the greatest amount of poverty but drew in the smallest amount of income from the poor rates. In the new order of things this seemed unfair, and so the two richer parishes were required to subsidise All Saints, to the extent that eighteen per cent of All Saints' revenues now came from the subsidies. Some families only needed a few pence a week to top up their income, others were given two shillings a week, or perhaps even more in times of sickness. At Christmas time food and clothing were handed out to the poor. The funds also helped with orphans, perhaps paying the costs of apprenticing them, and with paupers' funerals. In addition to the poor rates there were also special collections from time to time. In 1625 there was money over from the Fast Days for plague relief, so the surplus was invested in the Brewhouse. In times of poor harvests, when the price of grain shot up, the Dorset Justices of the Peace ordered the purchase of a quantity of grain which could be sold at a much lower price than was currently being realised in Dorchester market; this was in response to a general direction from the Privy Council but it was diligently carried out, to an extent not commonly found elsewhere.

Beggars and vagrants were treated firmly, but the 'deserving' poor were given practical help in various ways, including the supply of cheap fuel to assist in heating their homes. In 1618 it was decided to establish a Fuel House in the Hospital garden, and both Holy Trinity and St Peter's parishes gave money for the purchase of wood, which was then sold at a discount according to need. This had a side benefit for good order and the interests of local landowners, because a prohibition was introduced to stop people going out into the surrounding countryside looking for things to burn, 'they being well provided for fuel here'. It has be admitted, however, that some people were not impressed by the change, preferring still to go out to find free fuel, rather than buy it from the Fuel House.

Care for the sick was similarly enhanced above that generally provided in towns of a similar size to Dorchester. For those who could pay there were half a dozen physicians, a similar number of barber-surgeons, two families of apothecaries, as well as nurses and midwives. For the poor the parishes paid for nursing care, as well as making supplementary grants, and sometimes payments were made for more radical treatment – these included, for example, payment to a surgeon for the amputation of a leg, half to be paid at the time of the operation and the remainder when the patient was 'thoroughly cured'. In 1637 it was decided to set aside £10 a year from the Brewhouse funds to help with sick relief. Premises were acquired in the town to act as a temporary isolation hospital, for those suffering from serious infectious diseases, such as the plague.

Up until the time of the fire the only accommodation provided specifically for the elderly was the 'Old' Almshouse, near the Friary, now North Square; this was only for women. This institution was enabled to be brought up to date by endowments principally by Margaret Chubb but also by others. It accommodated ten women, whose costs were subsidised to an extent, but who still required support from relatives or parish funds. The other major benefactors who responded to the new social awareness in the town, whose names are still remembered today, were Sir Robert Napper and John Whetstone. Napper began building an almshouse in South Street in 1615, a building that still stands as 'Napper's Mite', built 'to the honour of God'. This was designed to take ten men, four from the country and six from the town. John Whetstone, who came from Rodden, near Abbotsbury, left £500 in his will for the 'building of an almshouse for poor folk'. After his death in 1619 a house was acquired in All Saints parish in what is now Church Street, also land to produce an annual income of £10, with the residue invested in the Brewhouse, for another £10 a year. This was intended for married couples, although survivors were allowed to remain after the death of a spouse. There were sufficient funds here to enable residents to live here without further help from their parish. These are the only significant legacies remaining today from John White's day, the three almshouses still being commemorated by name in the Dorchester Municipal Charities, with newer accommodation now being maintained in West Walks.

All this provided reasonably comprehensive social care in the town, certainly far exceeding the norm for the times. Dorchester was also remarkable for the way in which the inhabitants responded to appeals to help those in need elsewhere, not just in England but even further afield, this in addition to the raising of large amounts for major local projects, such as the Hospital and the Brewhouse. In 1620 over £120 was raised to go towards the defence of the Palatinate in Germany, where the Protestants were being besieged by Catholic armies. Nearer to home, in 1626 most of the collection of £100 went towards plague relief in Bridport. The generosity of folk can be seen from an example in 1640 when in a single week there were two collections, one to help plague relief in Taunton and the other to assist people made homeless by a fire in Yeovil, which together realised nearly £95, an average of nearly four shillings for every household in Dorchester. Evidence from other towns and cities of the time suggests a general response to this kind of appeal far below that found in Dorchester. The people's response to the crisis of the fire and John White's calls for a reformed social agenda clearly extended to wider philanthropy.

Writing in his work, '*The Tree of Life*', in 1647, John White looked back on what had been achieved in the town's response to the 'fearful fire':-

There met together about seven or eight well affected persons and agreed to contribute money, and annuities out of their lands, the sum of eight hundred pounds for the erecting of a Hospital, for the setting of poor children on work. The whole town consented to double their weekly rates for the relief of the poor, enlarged their churches and reduced the town into order by good government. What gained they by all this? Within the compass of six or seven years, God so poured his blessings upon the place, that it was in that short space in better condition than it had been before that calamity fell upon them.

On any assessment this was a remarkable transformation. John White does not refer to his own part in all this, or make any claims on his own account. There must already have been a general sympathy in favour of the puritan ideals for which he stood, and some of the initiatives might have been pursued without him. There is, however, an interesting reference in the Borough records to the early meetings after the fire, presumably those referred to in John White's piece above, to these meetings being 'assisted with our faithful pastor'. The image of pastor, a shepherd with his flock, is perhaps the best way to sum him up, with a lifetime committed to the care of the people in his charge, all of them whatever their circumstances.

If this could be achieved in Dorchester, what opportunities might there for replicating such a godly community elsewhere? For a man of vision the possibilities of helping new settlements to be established in the New World proved irresistible.

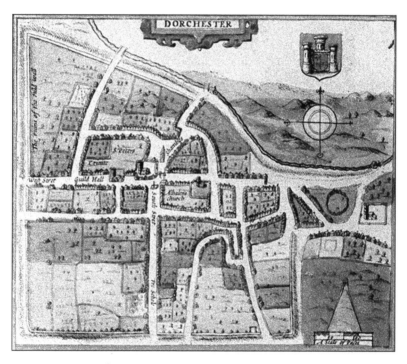

Map of Dorchester, Dorset by John Speed, 1611

John White (drawing by courtesy of Jo Duncan)

John White's Rectory, drawing by Eric Ricketts
(courtesy of Dorset County Museum)

John White's Rectory, Colliton Street, Dorchester, Dorset, 2017

St Peter's Church, Dorchester, Dorset

Napper's Mite, South Street, Dorchester, Dorset

Mary and John

Mary and John, cutaway model (courtesy of Dorset County Museum)

Roger Conant's House in Salem, Massachusetts

Seal of Dorchester, Massachusetts

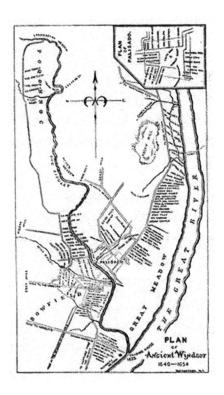

Map of Windsor, Connecticut, 1641-1654

Part 2

A New World
Across the Atlantic

4

The Dorchester Company

Over the previous century the English sailors had become used to crossing the Atlantic and exploring the coasts of North America. The fishing was especially good in the seas to the south of Newfoundland and English ships went there on a regular basis. At the beginning of the seventeenth century thoughts turned to establishing colonies on the mainland. The first of these was in Virginia, and in 1620 New England saw the arrival of the Pilgrim Fathers in the *Mayflower*. John White would have been aware of, and no doubt taken a keen interest in, all this. Merchants in Dorchester were trading through the harbour at Weymouth, and many of the fishermen based there carried out long voyages to catch cod and other fish, and perhaps also to do some trade in furs with the indigenous people. John White, however, would not have wanted to link up with the first colonists. Those in Virginia tended to belong to the High Church wing of the Church of England and were unlikely to be sympathetically inclined to the kind of puritanism practised in Dorchester. The Pilgrim settlement at New Plymouth, on the other hand, was largely made up of Separatists, people who could not put up with the Church of England at all, even the kind of moderate puritanism preached by John White, and who had left England altogether, first for the Netherlands and now for the New World, in order to 'do their own thing' free from persecution.

John White pondered over the life of the Weymouth fishermen sailing on a regular basis to the New World. 'Being usually upon their voyages nine or ten months in the year they were left all the while without any means of instruction', by which he meant guidance in matters of religion. Furthermore, the ships were 'double-manned'; more men were needed than were required to sail the ships across the Atlantic and back again, in order to fish the American waters and salt the catch down for the journey back to Europe. What if a settlement was established on the coast of New England, where the spare men could be left behind to form the nucleus of a colony? They would be on the spot for the next year's season, and in the meantime they could grow crops, tend cattle and find other food locally to feed themselves and the sailors returning in the spring, as well as making salt from seawater and keeping the fishing gear in repair. A minister could also be appointed to have pastoral oversight of this little community which could grow into the kind of godly commonwealth being experienced in Dorchester. This was the vision. One might perhaps want to criticise White for being naïve, in thinking that men recruited as fishermen could turn their hands equally to farming, and in beginning the enterprise with an inadequate financial base, but equally he must be praised for pushing ahead while the majority merely talked, and for persisting until success was achieved.

The Council of New England had put in place a procedure to be followed for the establishment of new settlements by English groups. An initial authority could be granted for the occupation of land as long as it was at least 10 miles from the nearest English settlement, or separated by a river. It was also possible to obtain a licence to allow a wider area to be assessed to identify a suitable location. If the initial occupation proved successful within a period of 7 years, then the original indenture could be exchanged for letters or grants of incorporation, which gave a formal constitution to the new community, with some powers of local government. Up until 1622 you had to be a member of the Council to apply, but then there was a change, so that others could also be considered, 'provided they be persons of honour or gentlemen of blood, except six Western Merchants'. This gave John White the opening he needed. He already knew some merchants who would qualify and it was not difficult to find some 'gentlemen of blood', who together would form the nucleus to promote his chosen project.

One of the 'Western Merchants' was Richard Bushrod. He was based in Dorchester and he agreed to front the application for a licence, as the first step to founding a colony in New England. Then Sir Walter Erle, of Charborough in Dorset, took over the leading role and chaired a formal meeting to promote the scheme locally. There the great prospects for investors were outlined: the possibilities for the grant of land in the new colony, opportunities for local unemployed, especially the young, to find work, a potential market for clothes etc, access to commodities such as timber, flax, hemp and dye-stuffs. Finally there was a call to Christian mission, 'how to settle the Christian faith in these heathenish and desert parts of the world'. The initial response was sufficiently positive for a subsequent meeting to choose a committee to oversee the new enterprise with Sir Walter Erle named as Governor and John Humphrey of Chaldon, near Dorchester, as Treasurer. Before long about 120 people had subscribed to the Dorchester Company, including 50 Dorset gentry, 30 merchants, mostly from Dorchester, and 20 clergymen. Over £30,000 was raised, which was judged sufficient to launch the project.

The first major expenditure was the acquisition of a small ship, of about 50 tons, *The Fellowship*, which was equipped and sent out with a full crew, plus the extra men who could be left to over-winter in New England. Unfortunately, by the time everything was ready, they were running about six weeks late in the season and they missed the best of the fishing. Nevertheless they carried on with the original scheme and left 14 men at Cape Ann, at the northern limit of Massachusetts Bay (now Gloucester) before sailing to Spain to sell their cargo of salt cod, albeit at a poor price. The next year they bought a second ship, a Flemish fly-boat of about 140 tons, which they tried to adapt to their purposes by the addition of a second deck. This was something of a disaster, because the alterations made the ship top heavy, and further refinements had to be made before the ship was safe to sail across the Atlantic. So again the best of the fishing was missed, with the inevitable impact on profitability, but this time 32 men were left at Cape Ann, together with cattle, food and equipment to help them through the winter. For the third season they added an extra ship but once more they were hit by bad luck. One of the ships sprang a leak on the ocean crossing and had to return to Weymouth. and the market for fish in Spain collapsed because of war between the two countries.

The Company was now running out of money, and there was no immediate prospect of it making any kind of profit in the short term. John White himself acknowledged fundamental weaknesses in his original concept. 'The very project itself of planting by the help of a fishing voyage can never answer the success that it seems to promise.' They had not so far identified a location that provided both a good base for the fishermen and suitable land for agriculture; Cape Ann was acceptable to the fishermen but it offered poor conditions for those who were expected to live there year round. Then there proved to be a skills issue as well. The settlers had been chosen primarily because they were fishermen and thus able to provide the extra help needed during the fishing season. But they were not farmers and they found it difficult to adapt to a life devoted to the care of crops and animals. It came down to the fact that the Company had been trying to achieve its aim of establishing a settlement 'on the cheap'. To be successful a settlement had to be made up of all the elements of a rural community, with fishing just one element among many. That was more than the Company could afford on the basis of the money raised so far.

However, not everyone currently at Cape Ann wanted to give up and come home. The numbers had been added to by some folk who had started out with the Pilgrim Fathers at Plymouth but who had not settled under their stricter form of puritan life and had either left of their own volition or been told to leave. They had travelled up the coast where they came into contact with the Cape Ann settlement. Roger Conant was described as 'a religious, sober and prudent gentleman', and he also happened to be the brother of John Conant who was well known to John White. His reputation and relationship were sufficient for John White to identify him as a potential leader for the settlement and he resolved to 'commit to him the charge of all their affairs, as well fishing as planting'. Another in this group was the Reverend John Lyford, who was invited to be their minister. Both, no doubt, fell into the category of what John White described as 'a few of the most honest and industrious' who decided to 'stay behind and take charge of the cattle sent over the year before, which they performed accordingly'. Roger Conant, in particular, did not want to leave New England, but did not feel that Cape Ann was the best place to develop and he suggested to John White a move to what he considered to be a more promising location, at a place called Naumkeag, which in due course would be renamed Salem.

The new site was on a neck of land, with the sea on both sides, either of which would provide anchorage for visiting ships. The area where they built their first houses was rocky, but there was land nearby with good enough soil to grow crops and pasture the cattle, with woods for timber and where pigs could forage when they were not eating clams from the shore. They began to establish a settlement, and most of the group were hopeful of making a home here. A few, however, were not so sure, including Mr Lyford, their minister, who decided to move south to Virginia. Roger Conant later claimed, probably correctly, to have been primarily responsible for keeping a small community together there. As he put it, 'When in the infancy thereof it was in great hazard of being deserted I was the means, through grace assisting me, to stop the flight of those few that then were here with me, and that by my utter denial to go away with them, who would have gone either for England or mostly for Virginia but hereupon stayed to the hazard of our lives'.

Back in England, with the Dorchester Company in the process of being wound up, it fell to a smaller group to maintain some level of support for the settlers. John White was one, Roger Conant's brother John another, and Richard Bushrod and a few other Dorchester merchants supplied the financial muscle. A ship was dispatched in the spring with more cattle as well as, presumably, further men and equipment, and they found that the community had weathered the winter well enough. They welcomed the new arrivals and supplies but were disappointed at the lack of positive news about their future. They had hoped to be given formal authority to occupy their new site, without which it could have been open to others back in England to apply in their stead and force them to leave. Accordingly they sent one of their number, John Woodbury, with the ship on its return journey to England to plead that something be done urgently to make their position secure.

There were then about 20 people at Naumkeag/ Salem, and they busied themselves building houses (mostly based on wooden frames brought over from England) and developing the farm land as best they could, in the hope that by the following spring John Woodbury would return with better news. One or two of them, including Roger Conant, had their wives with them, and the Conants saw the birth of the first English child there, perhaps a sign for a happier future. In his old age Roger Conant recalled writing at this time to his friends back in England, recommending New England as a potential haven for religious refugees. This positive outlook was just the encouragement that John White needed.

5

The Massachusetts
Bay Company

John White was not about to give up on his hopes for establishing a model godly community in New England. The initial efforts had suffered from the effects of a degree of over-optimism and naivety, especially in sending out the first voyage part way into the season and in the ill-thought out conversion of their second ship the following year, but also from bad luck, especially in the collapse of the market for fish in Spain. For many of the investors in the Dorchester Company enough was enough and they wanted to extract themselves from the venture as cheaply as possible. However, something had to be done about the small group of settlers remaining at Naumkeag/ Salem under the leadership of Roger Conant, either to bring them back to England or transfer them to another group of investors. John White thought of a third alternative, namely to bring in new investors to add to those Dorset folk who were prepared to carry on. So those who remained loyal to the enterprise approached their friends and acquaintances, and John White busied himself 'conferring casually with some gentlemen of London'. According to his own account later he encountered a mixed response, but out of all the conversations sufficient funds were forthcoming from new investors to send out a ship with further supplies immediately to support the existing settlement and to plan a significant new initiative.

The promise of new investment was conditional on further volunteers being identified to emigrate to New England, together with a suitable leader for them. Somebody mentioned the name of John Endecott, 'a man well known to persons of good note'. There are different accounts of his background, but he seems of have the qualities they were looking for at the time. He was enthusiastic about the project and ready to take the necessary responsibility. As it subsequently turned out he was a man of strong opinions and inclined to be hot-tempered. His views on matters of religion were more radical than John White's and he later risked upsetting the uneasy relationship between the settlers and King Charles' Government in England by ripping the cross out of an English flag when Royal Navy ships were visiting Boston harbour, on the grounds that displaying a cross in this way was 'Papist'. For the moment, however, he seemed to be the best person to found a new colony on the old foundation. He was also able to put forward his own stake for the project and was listed as one of those to whom an indenture was granted for the formal establishment of a colony in New England. This grant covered all the territory between a line three miles north of the Merrimack River and another three miles south of the Charles River; these lines were then extended west all the way across the continent from the Atlantic to the Pacific Ocean. This area included the existing small settlement at Naumkeag/Salem, and so it was confirmed that the new company, now (in 1628) known as the New England Company, would succeed to all the remaining interests of the Dorchester Company. With the grant of a royal charter the following year the company would be referred to as 'the Company of the Massachusetts Bay in New England'.

John Woodbury returned to New England with the extra supplies arranged by John White, this time accompanied by his son. He came with a message of hope for the small group who had struggled through another winter. Their hold on the territory was to be made secure as part of the grant to the new Company, and the resources available to them by way of manpower and financial support were going to increase dramatically with the involvement of a significant number of wealthy London merchants. They waited eagerly, therefore, for the next ship to arrive. During the summer the *Abigail* sailed from Weymouth with John Endecott and his wife with further pioneers. Many of these new settlers were people employed by the Company to help generate more income and profits for the Company from the natural resources in the colony in terms of fish, crops, timber, furs etc. The ship's cargo included 2 pipes of Madeira wine (in total about 252 wine gallons), perhaps destined for the new Governor's table, as well as more practical supplies such as lead, nails, food including quantities of butter, clothing including three dozen hats, and munitions including gunpowder and 20 muskets.

According to John Woodbury's son, Humphry, writing later, John Endecott quickly indicated that as far as he was concerned his arrival was not a mere continuation of what had gone on before. He announced that the new Company had purchased the 'houses, boats and servants' from the Dorchester Company and he also identified a desirable house left at Cape Ann which he ordered to be dismantled and transferred to the new settlement. He also charged a premium on goods brought over and put only a very low valuation on beaver skins, for example, offered by way of exchange, thus allowing for an increased profit to the Company. He also tried to limit the scope of what kind of work the settlers could do, which brought the original band to the point of mutiny. Some of them, of course, had come from other New World settlements and regarded themselves as freelance pioneers rather than servants of any company, whether the Dorchester or the Massachusetts Bay. They were on the point of leaving to join a group elsewhere when John Endecott realised that he had to give some ground, and made just enough concessions to enable Roger Conant to persuade his followers to stay and make the best of the new regime.

Those in England trying to manage this new enterprise at a distance were dependent on news being brought by returning ships. This would have included formal reports and also letters from the settlers, supplemented no doubt by comments by the ship's captain and others. John Endecott's message was extremely positive; the location was good and the prospects excellent in terms of scope for a greatly enlarged community. Roger Conant, on the other hand, wrote more cautiously, reflecting the tensions between the old planters and the new arrivals. The Company as a whole was happy to progress plans for further development and looked to send out many more emigrants. John White supported this, but had some reservations as to the aims and objectives of the undertaking. Some of the backers seemed to be more interested in the 'bottom line', that is, the profit that they could make, rather than the welfare of the emigrants, to the point where they were losing sight of the religious vision which was John White's starting point (and as stated as the Company's principal object). There was also a concern that some of the new pioneers coming forward were turning out to have more radical 'Separatist' views than John White was comfortable with.

New interest in the venture was coming from Lincolnshire and East Anglia, both of which areas would produce people who would have a major influence on the way in which the Massachusetts Bay colony would develop. John Cotton was already an established minister in Boston, in Lincolnshire – a Puritan, but still for the moment able to remain within the Church of England. Like John White he encouraged others to emigrate to New England, but unlike him in the end decided to emigrate himself rather than suffer under the reforms of William Laud. East Anglia produced the man who was to turn out to be the greatest leader in the early years of the new colony, John Winthrop. At this time he was practising as a lawyer in London and he entered on the scene first as an interested onlooker but very quickly he came to be central to the new initiatives.

As a first response to John Endecott's report he was told to expect between two and three hundred new emigrants, with a hundred cattle and other supplies, all to arrive in the following spring (1629). He was also informed that the party would include two ministers, who 'shall be by the approbation of Mr White of Dorchester and Mr Davenport'. Five ships set sail, including the *Talbot*, the *George*, the *Four Sisters*, and the *Mayflower*. The fifth ship, the *Lyon's Whelp*, was of particular interest to John White because it carried about 40 emigrants whom he had assembled from Dorset and Somerset and 'specially from Dorchester and other places thereabouts'. These included the Sprague family of Fordington and of Upwey, who were personal friends of his. There were now enough people overall to split into two communities, with the larger part remaining in Salem and the others moving a short distance away to found a new settlement at Charlestown.

John Endecott and his group were just recovering from a difficult winter, with a lot of sickness on top of everything else. Some of the illnesses were so severe that they felt the need of more experienced medical help than was available in the settlement, and so they sent to Plymouth to ask if they their doctor could be sent over. This was agreed, and Dr Fuller came and treated the sick. However, he also took the opportunity of promoting the Separatist views of his settlement – he was one of those who had come over from Holland in the first wave of emigrants. He seems to have influenced John Endecott in particular, reinforcing his radical sympathies. And the Governor, in his turn, used his authority over the colony to make its institutions reflect this shift in emphasis.

In fact, there turned out to be four ministers among the new arrivals, but two soon left. There remained, first, Francis Higginson, whose words on departing from his home country reflected John White's own sentiments: 'We do not go to New England as separatists from the Church of England, though we cannot but separate from the corruptions in it; but we go to practise the positive part of church reformation, and propagate the gospel in America.' The other minister was Samuel Skelton, who was an associate of John Cotton and likely to be more radical in his opinions. It fell to these two to give a lead in developing regular forms of worship, and it was decided in the community that one should be the minister and the other teacher. An election was held, which resulted in Samuel Skelton being inducted as minister and Francis Higginson as teacher.

There were two other important arrivals, the brothers John and Samuel Browne. John was a lawyer and Samuel a merchant. They originated from Essex but both seem to be well known to John White, and generally they were seen as potential leaders in the community. It was therefore directed from London that both should become members of a new ruling Council, which would, of course, be chaired by the Governor. Each of them was allocated two hundred acres of land, which again should have secured for them a respected place in society. Before long, however, they were going to be in trouble with the ministers and the Governor.

Puritans were used to daily worship at home and this was presumably the practice in Salem. The ministers wished to add to this regular public worship. As a principle this was welcome and even the fact that the pattern of worship adopted by the ministers owed more to the freer kind of worship followed by the Separatists than the liturgies set in the Book of Common Prayer might have been tolerated without undue objection. But when it came to light that the Browne brothers had been using the services from the Book of Common Prayer they were called to account. They raised a spirited defence of their actions and accused the ministers of departing from the orders of the Church of England. In effect, they were arguing that if Puritans like John White and Roger Conant's brother could find it possible to remain within the Church of England, so too ought the ministers of Salem and Charlestown. The ministers tried to justify their actions and clearly there was a major disagreement within the colony. John Endecott was probably not the right man to seek to reconcile the conflicting parties, and he told the Brownes that there was no place for them in Massachusetts Bay and they should return to England.

Back in England the general consensus was that the Brownes had been badly treated. Letters were sent off to the Governor and separately to the two ministers in reasonably diplomatic terms but making it plain that they had overstepped the mark and that they should have handled the differences over forms of worship more sensitively and sympathetically. Further, the Brownes were offered compensation which reflected not just their financial stake but also something for the efforts they had put into the venture and the pain they had suffered from their treatment. Unfortunately this would not be the last instance of disagreement and conflict within the colony, and it was an early sign of the tensions that were perhaps inherent in the whole project. Individual participants were motivated by different aspirations, and when these were reinforced by strongly held religious beliefs, they became matters of principle, and any who held contrary opinions must be enemies of the truth. John White's approach in Dorchester was to show a broad degree of toleration, as with, for example, the introduction of a covenant in his churches. Folk were challenged to sign up to the covenant, but they were not excluded from taking communion if they did not. He believed that the exercise of powers of persuasion was better than to employ force.

At about this time a document circulated under the title, *Reasons for the Plantation in New England*. No authorship is indicated but it is generally considered that it owes much to John White, although his original draft may well have been revised by John Winthrop and possibly also Francis Higginson. It is of interest here because it highlights the motivation of those now in control of the Massachusetts Bay Company, as well as facing up to objections which were no doubt being raised by others.

The document begins with a call to mission by the Church, which John White has been concerned at times that has been found lacking in some of the early settlers: 'It will be a service to the Church of great consequence to carry the Gospel into those parts of the world'. This is especially important against the background of the religious wars in Europe and the increasing troubles within the Church of England, so that there is a growing feeling that 'God hath provided this place to be a refuge for many whom he means to save out of the general calamity'. Economic factors are also relevant, in that there is widespread unemployment in England, with the poor being regarded as a burden on society, whereas by contrast the New World offers a whole continent 'fruitful and convenient for the use of man', a place where the poor could find work and an opportunity for them to make a better life for themselves. A decline in moral standards means that it is becoming harder for 'good and upright' workers to make a reasonable living and for children to brought up to appreciate good learning and religion. The new colony offers Christians an opportunity 'to support a particular church while it is in its infancy' as part of 'a company of faithful people' and this will serve as an example to others. All in all this 'appears to be a work of God for the good of his Church'.

The document then goes on to address a number of objections that have been raised against the plantation project. In answer to the observation that the land has for a long time been possessed by others the point is made that the natives in New England 'enclose no land, neither have they any settled habitation, nor any tame cattle to improve the land by, and so have no other than a natural [that is to say, not a formal legal] right to those countries. So if we leave them sufficient for their own use, we may lawfully take the rest, there being more than enough for them and for us.' Practical issues associated with such a major uprooting are similarly addressed. Yes, the venture is attended with difficulties, but 'so is every good action'. Some of the early settlements have struggled to establish themselves, but generally the prospects look good if the emigrants have the right approach. 'No place of itself has afforded sufficient to the first inhabitants. Such things as we stand in need of are usually supplied by God's blessing upon the wisdom and industry of Man, and whatsoever we stand in need of is treasured up in the earth by the Creator to be fetched thence by the sweat of our brows.'

Inspired by this vision the Massachusetts Bay Company progressed its plans for what would become known as 'the great migration'.

6

The Mary and John

Before any new emigrants were sent out there were housekeeping matters to be settled in London and John White travelled up as necessary to play his part in these. These included making proper arrangements for both old and new investors in the venture and setting out the parameters for ongoing management generally. Oversight of future trade and merchandise would remain in London, but day to day government of the colony would lie in New England.

There was a feeling of urgency now to set in train as much as possible as quickly as possible. Once folk had committed themselves to the idea of emigrating they were eager to leave. Meetings were held in London in October 1629 to finalise arrangements in readiness for sailings in the following spring. John White was not able to attend all these meetings but he was in London for an informal gathering to settle the Agenda for a session of the General Court. One of the items agreed to be included was 'to choose the Governor and Assistants for the Government in New England'. This was not in fact the proper way to proceed under the terms of the Charter, and no-one appears to have consulted John Endecott, the current Governor, but those who were present at the General Court (not including John White) carried on anyway. John Endecott was not even nominated and John Winthrop, who was now becoming the natural leader, was elected Governor, plus eighteen Assistants, of whom half would remain in London and the remainder sail to the New World.

John White was going along with the major initiative, but he seems to have some reservations as to the direction John Winthrop was likely to lead the new group of settlers. He was already disturbed about the treatment given in Salem to the Brownes and the obvious desire of some folk to impose a form of worship and church life that excluded those who did not accept it fully, so that the community was becoming more like the Pilgrim Fathers in Plymouth, who wanted to be totally separate from the Church of England. John White wanted to encourage his own, more moderate and tolerant, approach, and this explains why he formed his own group to establish a settlement following his ideals and why, when he asked ministers to go with them, they were indeed Puritans, as he was, but also, as he was too, still officiating as ministers within the Church of England.

He also had an idea as to where this new settlement could be based. The Sprague family, who had left Fordington, just outside Dorchester, to sail on the *Lyon's Whelp*, had begun their new life in Salem but had soon moved on with the Reverend Francis Bright (a moderate in John White's mould) to a new location at the mouth of the Charles River (to become Charlestown), before exploring further upriver to what would become Watertown. This was the area that John White now targeted.

As lay leaders he had two of those recently appointed Assistants of the Company. These were Roger Ludlow of Maiden Bradley, Wiltshire and Edward Rossiter of Combe St Nicholas, Somerset, both within his sphere of influence. Both were keen to be part of his new project and Roger Ludlow provided a ship to take the emigrants across the Atlantic. This was the *Mary & John*, a substantial ship for those days of about 400 tons and probably chosen as the most suitable vessel to make the crossing on its own, rather than as part of a convoy where smaller ships could help one another. Although English ships were crossing the Atlantic on a regular basis, it was still a hazardous voyage, not only for the storms that were frequently encountered but also for the risk of attack from hostile privateers, including the Spanish ones based at Dunkirk and even Turkish pirates. Thus, one of the Winthrop fleet, the *Warwick*, a ship of about 80 tons, never made it to the rendezvous with the others and was presumed to have been captured by the Spanish.

The two ministers chosen by John White were John Warham and John Maverick. John Warham's family had extensive Dorset connections, but he himself was born just over the Somerset border at Crewkerne. In 1627 he is found serving the church in Crewkerne when he received a formal reprimand from William Laud, then his diocesan bishop, for expressing puritan views in his preaching. To avoid further confrontation he took up an offer from the Bishop of Exeter, who was was sympathetically inclined towards him, to serve one of the Exeter churches until he resigned in order to set sail in the *Mary and John*. John Maverick may well already have been known to him as rector of the church in Beaworthy in North Devon. He too seems to have resigned from his living specifically in order to join the colonists. His eldest son, Samuel, had settled in New England a few years before so there was already a precedent in the family, although they did not join up once the rest (John's wife and their remaining six children travelled with him) had emigrated.

In total 140 migrants were recruited to join the expedition. They came from the three counties of Dorset, Devon and Somerset. Six families and a couple of single men left Dorchester, mostly from merchant families, no doubt inspired by their rector. There was a similar story elsewhere, four families from Bridport and the same from Beaminster as well as folk from the villages. In Somerset there was a focus of puritan zeal in Crewkerne where, of course, John Warham ministered until he got on the wrong side of Bishop Laud. In nearby Limington Roger Conant's brother, John, was rector, and was in touch with John White and a great influence in his locality. Similar links in Devon also produced potential emigrants. They were mostly of the 'middling sort', not from the upper classes, though some of them might just about aspire to be part of the gentry, and neither from the very poor, but rather merchants and skilled tradesmen with a few servants. Generally they believed that they had something positive to contribute to the project and saw this as an opportunity to invest in a new land to create something worthwhile in itself, as well as a better life, if not for themselves – they knew it would be tough to begin with – then for their children and children's children. All these assembled in Plymouth where the *Mary and John* was being prepared for the journey, and John White himself travelled down to see them off.

Captain Squibb was the master, with specific instructions as to his route and his ultimate destination. He was to take the northerly route across the Atlantic towards the fishing grounds of the Grand Banks south of Newfoundland before following the line of the coast south until he reached the mouth of the Charles River. There he was to go a short distance up river to the landing identified as the preferred place for the new settlement. They set sail from Plymouth on 20 March 1630. We do not have any record of their voyage, except that it took 10 weeks. This was not a particularly fast crossing and they may well have been hampered by head winds and even storms. Most, if not all, of the emigrants will have been very sea sick, at least for the first part of the trip until they got their 'sea legs', because the ship will have pitched and rolled violently in the swell. At least, however, they appear to have been spared the worst of disease which sometimes swept through the passengers crowded together below decks.

One of the passengers, Roger Clap, wrote many years later of their arrival in their new land. He was about twenty-one at the time of the emigration. He says nothing about the actual voyage, but records how Captain Squibb failed to take them up the Charles River but instead 'put us ashore and our goods on Nantasket Point, and left us to shift for ourselves in a forlorn place in this wilderness'. The new settlers clearly felt let down, and even betrayed by the

Captain's conduct. They knew that was not where they wanted to be, but they were not sure how to proceed and move not only themselves but all their equipment, materials and stores, as well as some animals, to a permanent location. In Captain Squibb's defence the entry into Massachusetts Bay was difficult and once inside the bay there were numerous islands, sandbanks and shoals to navigate around. His charts were probably sketchy, he did not have a local pilot to assist and his ship was larger than most that had previously sailed into the Bay. It was probably caution that stopped him from complying with the letter of his instructions. He did not sail back straight-away and the ship was still there when John Winthrop's ships arrived, so he may have waited for the opportunity to sail back to England as part of a flotilla. John Winthrop tried to soothe over the bad feeling between the captain and his passengers, and Captain Squibb fired off a farewell salute when he finally set sail as a gesture of encouragement, though how this was received is not recorded; certainly a residual bitterness is still evident in later recollections.

Roger Clap was part of a small group that set out to see if they could find their desired destination. There was a boat not far away, that belonged to old planters, and they were able to use this to explore up river. They made sure they were well armed and they took some goods with them. They first reached Charlestown where they found some wigwams and a house. There was a man in the house who gave them some fish to eat before they set off again to go further inland. The river grew narrow and shallow and they decided to stop and land their goods (Roger Clap says 'with much labour and toil, the bank being steep'). This was in the vicinity of what would become Watertown. There appear to have been some old planters about, because someone informed them that there were three hundred Native Americans nearby. This understandably made them nervous, but one of the old planters, who could speak the local language, went to the Native Americans and 'advised them not to come near us in the night'. Lookouts were posted, including

Roger Clap, but there was no trouble. The next day some of the Native Americans appeared and to begin with stood a little way off and merely looked at the new arrivals. A bit later some came closer holding out a large fish, which the English traded for a biscuit cake and everything seemed to be on a friendly basis.

In the meantime others of the main party had been exploring along the coast and they thought that a place, which they found out was called Mattapan by the Native Americans, looked promising. In particular the neck of land sticking out into the Bay would be good for grazing cattle, because they could be kept together with the minimum of fencing, there looked to be sheltered anchorages, and there was rising ground on the mainland where they could build their houses. Again, the local Native Americans seemed to be friendly. When the first group returned it was agreed that Mattapan would be their new home. Some kind of deal was done with the local Native Americans to confirm their rights to settle the land. And so they arrived at what would soon be renamed Dorchester.

A month later Governor John Winthrop arrived at the Charles River with his small flotilla of ships. They landed at Salem and first investigated Charlestown as a possible location for their settlement before deciding that the principal town should be built on neck of land known as Shawmut, which they renamed Boston. In this way both groups reminded themselves and their successors of their origins, one linked to the home town of their mentor and inspiration, John White, and the other to a major Puritan centre in Eastern England.

All the new arrivals quickly learned that they had arrived too late to plant any crops that year, and John Winthrop sent back to England an urgent request that they would need substantial supplies of food as soon as possible, although he had to accept that this would not be until the new year. Now they had to to their best to survive the worst of this winter. Roger Clap records that even the existing English population 'were very destitute when we came ashore', which meant that they could not expect much help from that quarter. The supplies they had brought with them would only last for a limited time, and their immediate need was to clear some ground and make sure that everyone had some better protection than the flimsy tents they relied on initially. They also built boats so that some of their number could go fishing.

They had brought some timber frames for houses, intended only for the leaders and richest in the community. For the rest people tried to upgrade their canvas tents to Native American-style wigwams or created dugouts in the earth with a roof of timber framework with a hole to let the smoke out from their fire. It must have looked like a modern make-shift refugee camp, albeit with a few proper houses standing among the shacks. Most of them had scant protection against the winter cold, with bare earth floors, and there was a constant risk of any timber framework being destroyed by the fire getting out of control, with all the nearby water frozen solid so that they had no means of putting out the fire.

In a new land they saw danger everywhere. They were afraid of rattlesnakes, marauding wolves threatened their cattle and there were other strange animals which they glimpsed in the undergrowth as they foraged for food and timber. To begin with they were also plagued by mosquitoes. They could not converse freely with the Native Americans, which must have made them apprehensive as to how long the initial friendliness would last.

But the biggest problem was food. Everyone was desperately hungry, and they had to eke out what little food they had or could get hold of, as in times of famine. They had no corn of their own and they were unable to find much to eat in the territory around them. Lack of fruit meant that nearly everyone went down with scurvy and lives were only saved by getting word to the folk at Plymouth, who sent over their physician, Samuel Fuller, to treat them as best he could. He brought some remedies and also let blood, a common treatment of the time. They managed to trade with the local Native Americans for some baskets of corn (not the kind of corn they were used to, but rather American maize); this helped but it did not go very far. Roger Clap recalled how 'Bread was so very scarce that sometimes I thought the very crusts of my father's table would have been very sweet unto me. And when I could have meal and water and salt boiled together, it was so good, who could wish better?' Later on they would discover game in the woodland nearby but for now their best hope of survival lay with the sea's harvest of clams, mussels and fish.

The new name, of Dorchester, for the settlement was confirmed by a decision of the Court of Assistants on 7 September 1630, as were the names of Boston and Watertown. To begin with Dorchester was very much under the care of the two ministers and formal steps for arranging for the government of the settlement were not taken until the following year. Building of a meeting house also had to wait until then and worship for the time being was presumably in the open air or in one of the bigger houses. There are indications that the church fellowship was becoming established and Roger Clap records that he was admitted into membership during the first year.

The autumn weather was relatively kind, with 'fair, open weather, with gentle frosts in the night'. Then, on Christmas Eve, it suddenly became cold, with snow and a driving wind. Within a matter of a couple of days the rivers were frozen over and everyone retreated indoors and kept themselves as warm as they could. This was when the enormity of the challenge they had taken on must have hit the new migrants particularly hard, although Roger Clap as an old man claimed that, 'I do not remember that ever I did wish in my heart that I had not come into this country, or wish myself back again to my father's house.'

Then relief came – earlier than they could realistically have hoped. The *Lyon* arrived off Nantasket on 5 February 1631, with about 200 tons of cargo, all in good condition. The Governor was taken out in a small boat to greet the ship and went aboard as it sailed into Boston through drifting ice. He then made sure that the provisions were distributed fairly with an allocation to each of the settlements around the Bay. It must have seemed that the worst was now over and things could only get better as everyone joined in a day of thanksgiving.

Part of this relief had been funded by John Winthrop as Governor, and his contacts back in England purchased the supplies and arranged for their delivery to the ship. Almost an equal amount, however, was raised due to the personal efforts of John White who, after hearing of the plight of the settlers, arranged for the necessary Government licences for the transport of grain to Bristol and Weymouth and secured funds from donations and collections to meet the immediate costs, much of it from Dorchester and the surrounding countryside.

More ships arrived during the year bringing essential supplies and responding to urgent requests from individual settlers. In Dorchester the principal objective was to transform their 'refugee camp' into something that resembled as near as possible the kind of village they had left behind in England. They had pitched their tents on elevated land above the shore, where there were fresh, clear springs, and now they replaced their tents with wood-framed houses, each with an acre or two of kitchen garden land for growing vegetables and planting the fruit trees they had brought with them and with space for outbuildings. In these gardens they could plant the cabbages, turnips, carrots, parsnips and herbs they had brought with them from England and also could experiment with growing the maize in the manner learnt from the local Native Americans. Soon there was something that looked more like a village street.

They helped each other as necessary and together tackled the communal projects of building a meeting house and clearing the first of what would become four large fields, which would be cultivated on the open-field system rather than divided into smaller lots by hedging or fencing. Clearing the land of trees and shrubs was a major undertaking. Pigs were no doubt used to help turn the soil and keep the weeds down. Cattle were grazed on Mattapan Neck, which proved to be good for the purpose both in terms of available food for the animals and to keep them reasonably confined and safe from predators, but progressively livestock was taken out each day into the countryside further afield and brought back into the village at nightfall. They kept a large number of goats, these being easier to care for than sheep, and the folk tried to convince themselves that goat meat tasted as good as mutton.

What was termed the Old Harbour, where they had first landed, turned out to be too shallow for shipping and the stream did not contain much in the way of fish. Just to the south, however, was a location that looked more promising, with another useful peninsula, Fox Point, and a river, the Naponset, that offered better fishing and was deep enough for ships to moor.

Outside the immediate village land was allocated by the Massachusetts Bay Company according to laid-down criteria. Nominally all land was held by the Crown, as in England, although the settlers took care to ensure that proper agreements were entered into with the local sachem, or chief – from the outset the new arrivals took into account John White's objective to preach the Christian Gospel to the Native Americans and his view that they should be treated with respect as fellow human beings under God.

The local allocation was determined by the Court of Assistants. In Dorchester the two Assistants, Roger Ludlow and Edward Rossiter, were granted farms of 100 acres each, close to the Naponset River; Edward Rossiter died in the autumn after their arrival but his allocation was passed to his son, Brian. Henry Wolcott, Thomas Newberry and Israel Stoughton, as investors, received similar allocations. Thomas Newberry, for example, ended up with a substantial plot for his house, forty acres of adjacent land, forty acres of marsh, plus 100 acres of upland and 100 acres of meadow on either side of the Naponset River; this reflected the size of his investment in the Company, his social standing and his large family, all relevant criteria. Israel Stoughton, in addition to a land allocation of 150 acres, received a most valuable right to build a water-mill for the community. For the rest, most of whom had paid for their passage out but had not put up any other money, there were smaller allocations, with a basic 50 acres, which again might be increased in the light of the size of a man's family, his social status and taking into account any servants he might have brought with him.

So, gradually, order was being imposed and the inhabitants of the new Dorchester faced up to the future positively and in good heart.

7

The Massachusetts Colony Grows

John White continued to encourage West Country folk to commit themselves to a new life in the colony at Massachusetts Bay. Some twenty ships a year made the journey across the Atlantic full of migrants. By 1635 the population of Massachusetts Bay as a whole had increased to over 8000. There is no total number for Dorchester at this time, but we know that the heads of families and individuals who had been granted land had risen to 130 and a significant proportion of these, possibly about half, had West Country origins, many from Dorset and even John White's Dorchester. Some of the new arrivals had responded to invitations from a relation who was already there; Roger Clap, for example, sent a letter back to England pressing his brother and his two sisters, with their husbands, to come and join him, which they all did.

The new Dorchester was becoming a town, and this was reflected in its new buildings and structures. First and foremost there was the meeting house. This was built towards the north end of the settlement, near to the Old Harbour. It was a reasonably substantial structure, with a thatched roof, and big enough for everyone to gather together for worship on a Sunday. Typically conduct of worship was shared between the minister and the teacher. The minister began the service with prayer, perhaps for a quarter of an hour, after which the teacher read and expounded a Bible passage. After the singing of a psalm the minister preached a sermon (probably at length), and the service ended with a final prayer and blessing from the teacher. During the week there were lectures, which were extended expositions of passages of Scripture. Once a month Sunday worship included the celebration of the Lord's Supper. In this way they continued their puritan pattern of corporate devotions, and they became increasingly appreciative of the fact that they could do this as news came to them of the restrictions and even persecution of Puritans back in England.

The two ministers and the two ruling elders, William Rockwell and William Gaylord, were the church authorities and for a time were effectively the town government, allocating lots for houses, imposing rates to pay for the maintenance of roads and bridges and ensuring that all the routine responsibilities that belonged to the community as a whole were properly carried out.

The meeting house also doubled as a community hall, and it was here that matters of business affecting the town were discussed and agreed. In the early days it also provided security for the settlers, who could take refuge together if they were nervous about a possible incursion by Native Americans or a threat of attack from pirates or Dutch warships. Guns and ammunition could be stored there and a sentry was posted on guard every night. Some years later a fortification was constructed so that guns could cover the mouth of the Neponset River and the bay in general. This provided better protection against attack from the sea, although the major fortification lay to the north, almost on the border with Boston, on what became known as Castle Island. This was first fortified in 1633 with mud walls, which Roger Clap says 'stood divers years' before being replaced with a structure made of Pine trees and earth, and finally in his lifetime by a small castle built with brick walls.

It was part of everyday life for the men to train as citizen soldiers. Most of the officers were also amateurs and they relied on one or two professional soldiers with real fighting experience to train them.

Dorchester had Captain John Mason, who had seen active service in the Netherlands, and he became responsible for the local militia, which basically consisted of all able-bodied men between the ages of sixteen and sixty. The company captain was Israel Stoughton, who seems to have had some military experience and would in due course return to England to serve in Oliver Cromwell's New Model Army. In the colony at large there were three regiments. Dorchester was part of the Suffolk County Regiment, of which Governor Winthrop was Colonel; as the oldest town its company was the senior one in that regiment.

They trained once a month and modelled themselves on what they had known in England, although they abandoned any reliance on the traditional twelve-foot pikes. Instead they were equipped with muskets, cumbersome weapons difficult to load and fire, and they had to practice firing their guns by ranks, then wheeling off to reload while the next rank fired. In readiness for encounters with Native Americans they wore padded corselets as a protection against arrows. Training days opened with a prayer from one of the ministers but ended with a drink or two together, which no doubt helped to bind the community together.

The other non-domestic building was the mill, the first in the colony. In accordance with the rights granted to him as part of his allocation Israel Stoughton constructed a weir across the Naponset River to create sufficient power to drive the mill and he also had a monopoly to net the alewives, a North American species of herring, as they swam upstream, on condition that he sold them to the plantation at a fixed price. To have such a monopoly on top of his trade as a miller made him a rich man.

The meeting house and the mill house are commemorated in the Corporate Seal of the town of Dorchester adopted in 1865. The fact that the attention of the founders of the town was focused on the church is marked on the shield by 'the rude, thatch-roofed church... without a chimney'. Israel Stoughton's water-mill 'is symbolically noted by the rude mill, with its large wheel, which is seen upon the left bank of the Naponset River' There is also included in the shield a representation of the free school, established in 1639, whilst in the background sit the Blue Hills, 'which served as a landmark to pilot the early settlers to the mouth of the Charles River'. The triple-towered castle surmounting the shield 'is adopted in respectful memory of Dorchester in Old England'. Finally, the motto, '*Pietate, Literis, Industria*' was chosen to signify that 'piety, learning, and industry were the prominent virtues which the early settlers coveted'.

Industry, in the sense of hard work, was vital to the development of a sustainable community. A major task involved the clearing of further agricultural land in the vicinity of the town, to create in the end four great fields. All the trees in these areas were removed, with the help of oxen to pull them over, as well as the scrub and weeds, until the field met the traditional English standard. It was only later that they learned to follow the Native American custom to ring the trees first to make them die, so that removing them once dead became easier. Then strips within the fields were allocated to individual families to plant and maintain, in accordance with an overall scheme of rotation of crops determined centrally. Some of the private fields were at a distance from the town, to the point where some of the men preferred to camp out in the fields for days at a time in the summer rather than trudge daily back and forth along primitive tracks.

The amount of livestock was increased by further imports from England as well as from breeding. Animals were valuable, many being lost on the voyages over, but numbers grew to a point where Mattapan Neck was unable to provide enough grazing for all the cattle and it was then restricted to beef cattle, with the cows being brought to assembly points each day, in response to blasts on the cowman's horn, to be driven out to pasture and then returned at sunset. Milking was carried out twice daily and the women folk used some of the milk to make butter and cheese. Pigs, goats and sheep were also grazed on a communal basis, which saved on labour and offered better protection from wild animals. Back home the women also kept hens and geese. As winter approached some of the animals were slaughtered and salted down to keep, some of the meat being sold to produce income. Outbuildings sheltered those that were kept.

Keeping pigs under control seems to have been a problem, especially when they broke through fences to get at the growing crops. A rule was introduced imposing a fine on both the owner of the fence and the pig (although little pigs were excused). This clearly failed to eliminate all troubles, and after 1635 trespassing pigs could be impounded and sold if the fine was not paid promptly.

Many of the West Country men had been fishermen back in England, and they took readily to fishing in the Bay. Cod and mackerel were abundant, and fish was an important part of the settlers' diet, some, like the pork, being salted down for the winter. Lobsters and crabs, clams and oysters were also plentiful. Local shallops, open boats with a shallow draft designed for use in in-shore waters, were also used for trading with neighbouring settlements and also, increasingly, with the Native Americans, for furs etc.

Beyond the cultivated land there was food to be had from shooting wildfowl, deer, hares and rabbits, and firewood from the woods, to be brought back in sufficient quantities to keep them warm throughout the long winter. During the winter, when for much of the time they were unable to do much outside beyond feeding the animals and keeping the fences secure, they repaired their implements and perhaps made some new ones, and spun and wove the wool and flax and made new garments. Some people dug holes in which they stored blocks of ice to help keep food fresh in the following summer.

This pattern of life was replicated in the different settlements throughout the colony. In each community land was allocated to settlers in a similar way as was done in Dorchester. As time went on houses were built, more or less substantial according to the means of the owners, together with the associated outbuildings. A meeting house provided the focus for both religious and communal life and later a church building was erected. In Dorchester Nicholas Upsall opened the first tavern in the colony and another Dorchester immigrant, John Cogan, left that town to open the first retail shop in Boston. John Winthrop's settlement, called Boston after the notable Puritan town in England and the former home of a number of the migrants, quickly came to be the dominant centre. Boston and Charlestown (which became a settlement in its own right, despite the initial reservations) proved to be better ports than the Old Harbour at Dorchester and offered the regular transport links with the old country.

To begin with, all the leading citizens could meet together for general gatherings and to elect the Governor, deputy and assistants. However, as the other settlements grew in both size and number frequent meetings became logistically more difficult and a more structured arrangement was introduced. The basic electorate was made up of the freemen. These were chosen locally subject to a condition introduced in 1631 that each should be a member of one of the churches in the colony. Now the freemen all met together once a year, primarily in order to elect the magistrates. The magistrates, together with deputies elected locally by the separate towns, were responsible for enacting laws for the government of the colony. This combination of centrally elected officials and local representatives could give rise to tensions between the two groups, and the magistrates took upon themselves the right to exercise a veto on proposals by the deputies. The deputies then fought for, and eventually won, a similar negative influence. And so, by degrees, a formal constitution developed.

Locally the town meeting dealt with the day-to-day administration of the community. The 'selectmen' were chosen to hold office for just half a year at a time but could be re-elected. This body was now separate from the church, but church and town meeting generally worked in harmony for the good of the town at large. Nearly all continued to be motivated by similar ideals and where dissension arose the majority tended to band together to isolate those whom they identified as trouble makers. There were one or two notable casualties, including Roger Williams who left to found a new colony at Rhode Island and Anne Hutchinson who had the temerity to put herself forward as a woman preacher in a wholly male sphere. The prevailing views tended to become more rigid and intolerant, which led in due time to the infamous Salem Witch Trials.

A few settlers gave up and returned to England, bearing tales of starvation and illness. Others, however, reported back more positively, and it was not just people like Roger Clap encouraging other members of his family to join him. One of the sea captains, for example, Thomas Wiggins, wrote in 1632 to the King's Secretary of State, Sir John Coke, 'to clear the reputation of the plantation from false rumours spread abroad'. After highlighting the valuable natural resources the area offered he emphasised how industrious the settlers were and that they 'have done more in three years than others in seven times that space, and at a tenth of the expense'. He also commented that 'they are loved and respected by the Indians'.

It became clear that the colony was well established and had a long term future. Immigration continued and even increased and in 1635 over three thousand immigrants arrived. Among them was a young, but very well connected, individual, Henry Vane, whose father held high office in the court of King Charles, but who himself was a committed Puritan. It was one of the King's more astute moves, because he gave the young man, who was starting to be troublesome in England, a licence to spend three years in the Massachusetts Bay colony with a commission, along with John Winthrop's son, also John, to extend Britain's territories in North America by establishing a new colony in the area known as Connecticut. It was not really the King's fault that events did not work out as smoothly as he must have hoped, but his principal aim accorded with the feelings in the colony that it was time for many to move to pastures new.

8

Connecticut

Early in 1635 a number of Dorchester residents decided to leave their new settlement in favour of prospects further west. The leader of this latest venture was Roger Ludlow, who earlier had provided the *Mary and John* to bring over the migrants from the West Country assembled by John White, and some of his fellow migrants now prepared to accompany him once again.

Their objective was land on the banks of the Connecticut River, a little under one hundred miles away, and accessible from Massachusetts Bay either by land routes established by the Native Americans or round the coast by sea to the mouth of the river. This land appeared to offer much better farming land than the poor, stony ground around Dorchester. There were some Native Americans living in the area, but there seemed to be enough land for everyone, and the immigrants were prepared to come to a commercial agreement with the local Native Americans to acquire a suitable site for a new settlement. Another influx of arrivals in Dorchester was beginning to create competition for the available land there, and it was tempting to sell up their newly cleared ground and their houses in the hope of ending up with something much better.

The first Europeans to explore the Connecticut were the Dutch. In 1614 Adriaen Block sailed up the river as far as modern Hartford and it was decided to establish a trading post there to encourage trade with the local Native Americans. This post was later fortified, but the Dutch took no steps to colonise the area further, and although they attempted to dissuade the first English arrivals they had neither the strength nor the will to force the issue. The Earl of Warwick identified this as a potential area for settlement and obtained the necessary rights from the English authorities. He then passed on this so-called authority to Lord Saye and Sele and Lord Brooke, and it was they who organised the expedition under John Winthrop the Younger, backed by the commission from King Charles to young Henry Vane. When they sailed from England in 1635 they came with grandiose plans and the necessary materials and equipment to build a fort at the mouth of the Connecticut, a fort to be given the name from its sponsors of Fort Saybrook.

Meanwhile in Massachusetts Bay there was a feeling among some of the Dorchester residents, and others in the colony at large, that the ruling establishment was becoming too intolerant of views that did not accord closely with the favoured line. In particular, more people were supporting the independent kind of churchmanship that sought a decisive split from the Church of England. John White's pleas for moderation, in which he encouraged citizens to commit themselves to a covenant relationship in the church but not to exclude from a full role in the community those who were not ready to take this step, were being ignored as the Massachusetts society took shape. Rather than fight this locally, some moderates took the alternative route of seeking to implement their ideas elsewhere.

For Roger Ludlow there were also personal reasons. From the time of his arrival in the colony he had been one of the natural leaders. But he was working alongside other strong-minded men with whom he frequently clashed. He caused offence by his arrogant and overbearing manner and eventually he paid the price by being voted out of office. After a year as deputy governor he failed to be elected governor to succeed Thomas Dudley, and he was known as someone who tried to limit the power and influence of John Winthrop. In fact, he was not even confirmed in his role as a magistrate, and when, in a fit of pique, he offered to resign as overseer of the Castle Island fortifications the court not only accepted his resignation without question but also instigated an investigation into his management of the funds for the works. Life in a new territory offered an opportunity to re-establish himself as a leader and provide a more secure future for his family. That he could do this in furtherance of John White's ideals must have been an added attraction.

So, a small group of pioneers was gathered together, ready to reconnoitre possible sites for a settlement. Then, suddenly, there was a new sense of urgency. On 16 June a ship arrived in Boston from England, the *Christian*, bringing a group, under the leadership of Francis Stiles, in connection with the Fort Saybrook initiative. If they got there first, they might lay claim to the whole area and bar any prospects for the Dorchester group. The sea journey would be quicker than the overland route, but they managed to delay the new arrivals in Boston with welcoming formalities and the making ready of a suitable boat to go round the coast for long enough to allow Roger Ludlow and his group to get to the river first.

The route overland took them through swamps, rivers, forests and mountains, but also into a succession of Native American villages, where they were well received and helped on their way. Finally they arrived at the Connecticut River, about sixty miles from its mouth, at a place called by the local Native Americans Matianuck, where the River Tunxis joins the Connecticut. The Plymouth Colony had already established a trading post here and the small contingent in residence offered hospitality to the new arrivals while they decided where to settle. In fact, Roger Ludlow quickly decided that this was the best vicinity for them too, and he focused in particular on an area of river meadow with a bluff with an expanse of higher ground just above it, bordered by both rivers. The local Native Americans, the Podunks, had their own settlement on the other side of the Connecticut, but this was not seen as a problem and Roger Ludlow sent word back to Dorchester that he had found a new home.

It did not take long for others to arrive to stake their claims, and later in the summer a larger party of some sixty people arrived, many having come with horses, cows and pigs, all they had to establish their families, all brought along the narrow Native American trails, a journey which John Winthrop described in his diary as 'tedious and difficult'. It was now October and they set about making the best temporary shelters they could before winter set in. But winter came sooner than they hoped, and by 15 November the river was frozen over and impassable to shipping and the supply ships they had been expecting could not reach them. They were faced with a crisis almost worse than when they had first set foot in New England.

It was not realistic to hope that they could all survive the winter on what they had with them. Equally they did not want to abandon what looked to be the most promising location for their new Dorchester. It was decided that just a few men should remain to hold their position and look after the cattle. The rest had to return to Massachusetts Bay. The overland route was now also a hazardous proposition, especially for the women and children, and they took the only alternative, to follow the river down to the sea in the hope of finding a ship there to take them round the coast. They made it safely and were delighted to see a ship, not the one they were expecting but one nevertheless that would take them on board. The only problem was that the ship was stuck in ice. At least they were provided with food, and fortunately there was enough of a thaw for the ship to break free – only for it to run aground on a sandbank. Unloading some of the cargo enabled the ship to be floated off, after which the cargo had laboriously to be loaded again, but finally they set sail to safety.

Roger Ludlow, with a small group, made the difficult journey overland, losing one of their number on the way drowned under ice. Those left behind had a terrible time. Their food quickly ran out and they had to rely on what they could forage locally, even acorns. Most of their cattle died and their one consolation was that they had retained their hold on their chosen new home. Back in Dorchester there was some discussion about the merits of the whole enterprise – was it really going to be worth it? John Maverick was against carrying on, but he died during the winter and with his death the main reluctance faded. More immigrants had arrived in Dorchester putting greater pressure on resources there, and John Warham offered to lead a major group back to the Connecticut.

The planning went better this time. They set off as early as possible in the new year, to give time to plant and harvest crops during the summer. They also arranged to have heavy loads taken round by sea and up the river to the new settlement. There was a cost associated with this, 45 shillings a ton, but for those who could afford it, this was something worth paying to avoid the difficult overland transportation along the narrow Native American trails. Roger Ludlow was one of the first to arrive, before the end of April, to bring relief to those left there over the winter. Dorchester folk made up a significant proportion of the early arrivals, and they resolved to give this new settlement the same name of Dorchester. Over 50 of the families now setting up home here came from Dorchester Massachusetts and about 35 of these had come over from the West Country on the *Mary and John* or as part of another complement of migrants assembled under John White's fatherly eye. In 1637 the name of the settlement was changed to Windsor, which has continued to today.

The new arrivals had obtained the agreement of the local Native Americans to their presence but in colonial terms their status remained uncertain. The Dutch still held their trading post a little way downstream, although there were no signs that they had any serious intention of building a significant colony based on this. Of more immediate concern were the other English interests, namely similar migrations from Massachusetts, most notably that led by the Reverend Thomas Hooker, which founded Hartford, just next to the Dutch post, and the semi-official expedition acting under the patent from Lord Warwick and led by John Winthrop the Younger. It seems that the folk from Dorchester were regarded as interlopers, even trespassers, by both the other groups, but so far they managed to keep their rivals out of their chosen location.

There was clearly a mutual interest in creating some kind of formal co-operation between these groups and during the winter of 1635/6 private discussions were held in Boston between John Winthrop the Younger, Thomas Hooker and Roger Ludlow, presided over by the then Governor of Massachusetts, John Haynes. It was agreed to provide for all the English parties who had moved into Connecticut to settle and to establish a provisional government for the whole area in the form of a Commission of eight men, with Roger Ludlow to be the first Commissioner. Magistrates and deputies were to be elected, as in Massachusetts, except that here church membership was not imposed as a requirement for eligibility to vote.

Just about this time a new threat arose from some of the Native Americans. Generally relations had been good, with the English immigrants being welcomed by the native people and helped by them to settle in and learn the ways of the land. In return the English tried to deal fairly with them, in paying for the land which they occupied and in the terms of their mutual trading. The different Native American tribes kept to their own territories, and so the English came to deal with separate groups as they expanded their areas of occupation. However, one unforeseen import from the Old World was disease and many Native Americans succumbed, especially to chickenpox and smallpox. As a result many died and communities became depleted and weakened. A nearby tribe, the Pequots, saw an opportunity to enlarge their own territory and mounted an invasion. They were known for their brutality (soon to be matched by English armed forces) and the local Native Americans looked to their English neighbours for help in their resistance.

The story of the Pequot Wars is outside the scope of this account but this threat of Native American attack as well as the possibility of Dutch aggression made the need to construct fortifications to protect the community at Windsor a priority. Windsor's military commander, Captain John Mason, who had overseen the local militia in Dorchester, now saw to it that this town was properly defended. The bluff above the confluence of the Tunxis, now known as the Rivulet, with the Connecticut offered the best position. A wide area was enclosed by a ditch with an inner earth rampart. On the rampart a palisade of tree trunks was erected. They called it the Palisado, from the Spanish term for a semi-fortified town, a name that survives to today. It was a massive undertaking for the settlers, against so many other competing claims for their time and energies, but it meant that they were comforted by the knowledge that, if necessary, everyone could take shelter and be protected within it. Some years later their meeting house would be built in its centre.

Captain Mason and some thirty men left Windsor to join the forces against the Pequots and it was only towards the end of 1637, when that menace had been seen off, that the residents could set about establishing their settlement as a viable enterprise. The prospects were so much better than those offered by the land in Massachusetts Bay from which they had come. There were wide expanses of rich meadowland, good soil and easy to work, ideal for crops and cattle. It was not all so good for building on, however, as some found to their cost when their houses were flooded out in a spring flood in 1639, but there was enough higher ground for that purpose. There was even a rocky outcrop nearby, called Rocky Hill, where there was red sandstone to quarry to use in their buildings.

Home lots were allocated on a similar basis to that in Massachusetts Bay, with smallholdings surrounding house plots. There was a range of building skills available among the residents, with carpenters, bricklayers and stonemasons as well as blacksmiths, and in addition Matthew Grant was sufficient of a surveyor to help with the general layout of the town, including the roads. The houses were generally constructed with timber frames, a few with imported prefabricated parts but mostly from local oak and other wood. To begin with roofs were thatched, but the hot summers meant that fire was a real hazard and in time wooden shingles came to be the preferred material. The West Country kind of clunch infilling of the walls did not provide sufficient insulation for the very cold winters and the East Anglian style of weatherboarding was adopted instead. Chimneys were stone or brick. Size varied according to the means of the owner, except that the minister, John Warham, and later also Ephraim Huitt, were provided with substantial houses as befitted their status in the community. In addition John Warham was allocated various areas of prime agricultural land, as well as the right to tolls from the town's grist mill.

The town spread out on the west bank of the Connecticut (or Great) River and along both north and south banks of the Rivulet. There was a ferry across the Rivulet, with the ferryman appointed by the town, which also set rules and regulations for its use – no more than 35 passengers in the larger boat, 6 in the smaller, with precedence to be given to magistrates and elders on Sundays, presumably so that they would not be late for worship. Sunday services were held in the open air as long as the weather permitted it; otherwise folk squeezed into one of the big houses. The ferry across the Great River, as an important element of communications with the outside world, was operated under a franchise granted by the General Court. The townsfolk built their houses on both sides of the Rivulet. Some of the bigger houses, including Roger Ludlow's and John Warham's, were in the pleasant meadow on the south side of the Rivulet, close to the ferry, albeit at the risk of flooding. The Palisado was opposite and from there the new Main Street stretched out to the north parallel to the Great River. On Main Street families tended to gather together according to their place of origin in England, the first group containing sixteen families from the West Country, including ten from Dorset, from Dorchester and the Brit valley north of Bridport. Seven of these families had sailed in the *Mary and John*.

So the spirit of John White lived on and his legacy deserves still to be celebrated. In England his association with the Parliamentarians in the great dispute with King Charles I and participation as one of the Westminster divines led to his role being downplayed in the period of the Restoration of Charles II; in particular, the Act of Uniformity led to many Puritans of his mould being ejected from their churches and communities. In New England, however, his reputation remained high and the title of 'Founder of Massachusetts' acknowledges this. But we also need to remember that his influence did not stop there and it can clearly be traced in Windsor, Connecticut, and it continued to spread as his spiritual heirs migrated further into yet newer settlements. So John White's vision of a Christian commonwealth first realised in Dorchester in England was being fulfilled in the New World.

Further Reading

Rory T Cornish, 'White, John (1575-1648)', *Oxford Dictionary of National Biography* (Oxford University Press 2004)

David Underdown, *Fire from Heaven: Life of an English Town in the Seventeenth Century* (Harper Collins 1992)

Frank Thistlethwaite, *Dorset Pilgrims: The Story of West Country Pilgrims who went to New England in the 17th Century* (Barry & Jenkins, London 1989)

Ann Natalie Hansen, *The Dorchester Group: Puritanism & Revolution* (At the Sign of the Cock, Columbus, Ohio 1987)

Frances Rose-Troup, *John White, The Patriarch of Dorchester (Dorset) & The Founder of Massachusetts 1575-1648* (G P Putnam's sons 1930)

William Dana Orcutt, *Good Old Dorchester: A Narrative History of the Town 1630-1893* (Cambridge Mass. 1893)

Further information can be obtained online through the following websites:-

> www.dorsetcountymuseum.org
> www.dorchesterhistoricalsociety.org
> www.dorchesterathenaeum.org
> www.winthropsociety.com
> www.windsorhistoricalsociety.org

The 17th century texts quoted in this book are all available online.

Index

Lightning Source UK Ltd.
Milton Keynes UK
UKHW02f0011150318
319459UK00005B/77/P